SLIM & DELICIOUS
PASTA
COOKBOOK

Marjorie Trotta

Sweetwater Press
Florence, Alabama

Published by Sweetwater Press
P.O. Box 1855
Florence, Alabama 35631

Produced by The Triangle Group, Ltd.
227 Park Avenue
Hoboken, NJ 07030

Design: Tony Meisel
Special thanks to Risa Gary of Mikasa, New York
Origination and printing: Cronion S.A., Barcelona

Printed in Spain

ISBN 1-884822-02-9

Contents

Introduction

Pasta has fast become everybody's favorite meal. It's quick, it's easy and it's liable to more variations than you can sample in a lifetime.

Pasta can be divided into two basic categories—fresh and dry. Additionally, it can be made with eggs or without. It can be stuffed as with tortellini or ravioli or plain as with spaghetti, linguini or penne. In either case, it is usually sauced.

Most Americans think that pasta is usually heavily sauced with tomato variations. In Italy, however, sauce is usually applied sparingly, so as not to drown the natural taste of the noodles themselves. And, depending where in the country one finds oneself, the sauces are often not made with tomatoes at all.

The great thing about pasta is that it is made up mainly of complex carbohydrates. Therefore, it is naturally healthy and not at all fattening by itself. The sauce makes the difference. Butter, cheese (and even the Italians often overdo the cheese), meats and sausages will naturally add many, many calories to any dish of pasta.

But sauces of fresh vegetables, fish, shellfish, olive oil and stock make refreshing, healthy and delicious dishes in their own right.

If the pasta is to be only a first course, be sure that what follows contrasts with the pasta, in taste and texture and substance. In other words, if one is going to eat tortellini with a meat sauce, a main course of grilled fish would be preferable to one of *stufato*, or pot roast.

Finally, a word about preparing pasta. Always cook it in a large amount of water. Always salt the water, otherwise the pasta will be insipid. And always drain it and sauce it immediately. People wait for pasta, pasta does not wait for people.

Spaghetti with Oil & Garlic

1 pound thin spaghetti
2-3 tablespoons olive oil
5-6 cloves or garlic, finely chopped
salt to taste
black pepper to taste

Cook the spaghetti in a large pot of salted boiling water. Drain.

In a small skillet heat the oil. Add the garlic and quickly sauté until the garlic begins to brown.

Place the spaghetti in a serving bowl. Add the garlic and oil, toss. Season with salt and pepper. Serves 4.

Elbows with Fresh Herbs & Cheese

1 pound elbow macaroni
1/2 cup low-fat margarine
2 cloves of garlic, crushed
2 tablespoons fresh basil, finely chopped
1 tablespoon fresh mint, finely chopped
1/4 cup grated Parmesan cheese
1/4 cup grated Romano cheese

Cook the pasta in a pot of salted boiling water. Drain.

While the pasta is cooking, melt the butter in a skillet; add the garlic, basil and mint. Sauté for 1-2 minutes.

Add the drained pasta to the skillet and mix well until covered with butter and herbs. Add the cheeses and mix gently but quickly. Season with fresh black pepper. Serve at once. Serves 4.

Spaghetti with Tomato Sauce

1 pound spaghetti
2 tablespoons olive oil
3 cloves of garlic, finely chopped
2 pounds fresh tomatoes, chopped and seeded or
    1 large can imported Italian tomatoes, drained
1/4 cup chopped fresh basil
1/4 cup chopped fresh arugula
2 tablespoons chopped parsley
salt to taste
black pepper to taste
freshly grated Parmesan cheese, optional

In a large skillet, heat the oil. Add the garlic and sauté for 1-2 minutes. Add the tomatoes and cook uncovered over a low heat for 15-20 minutes or until the sauce begins to boil and thicken. Keep hot.

Cook the pasta in a pot of boiling salted water. Drain.

Add the basil, arugula and parsley to the sauce. Stir well. Place the pasta in a serving bowl. Toss with the sauce and season to taste with salt and pepper. Sprinkle with cheese if desired. Serves 4.

Pasta with Chicken Livers, Tomatoes & Garlic

1/2 pound fresh chicken livers
3 tablespoons olive oil
2 cloves garlic, peeled and chopped
1 large can imported Italian plum tomatoes, drained
1 teaspoon grated lemon peel
1 teaspoon fresh rosemary, chopped
2 tablespoons Marsala wine
1 pound bucatini or spaghetti
salt and pepper to taste

Clean the chicken livers and cut into small pieces.

Heat the olive oil in a saucepan and add the chopped garlic. Let brown lightly over medium heat. Add the tomatoes and mash roughly with the back of a wooden spoon. Add the lemon peel, rosemary, salt and pepper and let simmer for 15 minutes.

Cook the pasta in a pot of boiling salted water. Drain.

Just before serving add the Marsala to the sauce and simmer for 2 minutes. Pour over the drained pasta and serve immediately with grated Parmesan cheese on the side. Serves 4.

Rice Noodles with Peanut-Ginger Sauce

This refreshing dish can be served as an appetizer or as part of an Oriental buffet. The fish sauce and noodles can be bought in larger supermarkets and Oriental shops.

8 ounce package of Oriental rice noodles
1 tablespoon sesame oil
2 cloves garlic, finely chopped
1 green pepper, cored, seeded and julienned
1 red pepper, cored, seeded and julienned
2 scallions, coarsely chopped
1 tablespoon fresh ginger, julienned
4-6 ounces small, cooked shrimp
2 tablespoons *nam phua* (Thai fish sauce)
1 tablespoon soy sauce
1/4 cup smooth peanut butter

Place noodles in a large bowl and cover with boiling water for 5 minutes. In a saucepan, heat the sesame oil. Sauté the garlic, peppers, scallions, ginger and shrimp for 5-7 minutes over high heat, tossing constantly. Add the fish sauce, soy sauce and peanut butter and toss well. Drain the noodles well and place in a bowl. Pour the shrimp and vegetable mixture over and serve. Serves 4.

Macaroni & Cheese

The old stand-by with a new twist!

1 pound macaroni
3 tablespoons butter
3 tablespoons flour
2 cups warm 1% fat milk
1 cup grated low-fat cheddar cheese
1 teaspoon Tabasco sauce
1/2 teaspoon ground nutmeg
1 teaspoon black pepper
2 teaspoons salt

Boil the macaroni in at least 4 quarts of salted water until just firm. Drain and set aside. In a saucepan over low heat, melt the butter. Stir in the flour and blend thoroughly. Let cook 2 minutes. Slowly add the warm milk, stirring constantly, until well blended. Add the cheese and Tabasco and continue stirring until the cheese is melted and the whole mixture is smooth and thick. Place the macaroni in a deep, oven-proof casserole. Pour the cheese mixture over and fold in. Place in a 400 degree F. oven for 20 minutes until hot through and browned on top.
Serves 4.

Pasta with Tuna Sauce

An unusual combination, typical of the Ligurian coast of Northern Italy. It makes a fast, delicious meal, accompanied by a salad and dry white wine.

2 cloves garlic, chopped
1 7-ounce can tuna in olive oil
pulp from tomatoes
1 cup tomato juice made from Italian plum tomatoes
1/2 cup fresh basil leaves, finely chopped
1 teaspoon capers, roughly chopped
1 pound penne

First, make the sauce. Sauté garlic in the oil drained from the tuna. Add the tomato pulp and cook for two minutes over medium heat. Add the remaining ingredients, except the pasta and continue cooking for 10 minutes until well-blended and slightly reduced. Cook the penne in plenty of boiling, salted water until *al dente*, slightly resistant to the tooth. Drain pasta and immediately place in a heated, large bowl, add the sauce and toss thoroughly. Serve immediately. Serves 4.

Linguine with Clam Sauce

1/4 cup olive oil
1 medium onion, finely chopped
2 cloves of garlic, crushed
1 large can imported Italian tomatoes, drained, sieved
    and mixed with juices
1/2 teaspoon oregano
2 dashes of Tabasco sauce
2 dozen cherrystone clams, shucked and
    coarsely chopped, set aside in their juices
1 pound linguine

In a large skillet, heat the olive oil. Add the onions and
sauté for 5 minutes or until the onions begin to wilt and
become transparent. Add the garlic and cook 1 minute
longer.

To the onion mixture add the tomatoes, oregano, and
Tabasco; bring the mixture to a boil. Lower the heat to a
simmer and continue cooking for 8-10 minutes or until the
mixture begins to thicken and reduce.

Add the clams with their juices to the skillet cook over
a low heat for 3-5 minutes.

Cook the linguine in a large pot of boiling salted
water. Drain.

Transfer the linguine to a serving bowl and toss with
some of the sauce. Spoon the rest of the sauce over the
pasta. Serves 4.

Spaghetti with Broccoli, Garlic & Oil

1 pound or 1 large bunch of broccoli
1/4 cup olive oil
4 cloves of garlic, finely chopped
1 pound spaghetti
freshly grated Parmesan cheese, to taste
black pepper, to taste

Cook the spaghetti in a large pot of salted boiling water. Drain.

While the spaghetti is cooking, trim the broccoli and break the bunch into florets. Steam 8-10 minutes or until just tender.

While the broccoli is cooking, heat the oil in a large skillet. Add the garlic and sauté briefly. When the broccoli is done, add it to the garlic oil mixture, sauté for 1-2 minutes.

Place the garlic and broccoli mixture in a large serving bowl. Add the spaghetti and toss. Sprinkle with cheese and pepper to taste. Serves 4.

Spaghetti with Olives, Tomatoes & Anchovies

1/4 cup olive oil
2 cloves of garlic, finely chopped
1 can of anchovy fillets, finely chopped
1 large can of imported Italian tomatoes, drained and
    coarsely chopped, reserve juice
10-12 imported black olives, pitted and coarsely chopped
1/4 cup fresh basil, coarsely chopped
1 pound of spaghetti
black pepper to taste

In a large skillet heat the olive oil and stir in the garlic and anchovies. Cook until anchovies begin to disintegrate; about 2 minutes. Add the tomatoes and some of their juice, the olives and basil. Simmer the mixture over a medium heat, stirring occasionally, until the sauce thickens only slightly.

While the sauce is simmering, cook the spaghetti in a large pot of salted boiling water. Drain.

Transfer the spaghetti to a serving bowl and toss with the sauce. Season with pepper to taste. Serves 4.

Linguine with Seafood & Basil Cream

2 tablespoons butter
2 cloves garlic, peeled and chopped
1/2 pound shrimp, cleaned and deveined
1/2 pound scallops, cut in halves or quarters if large
1 cup fresh basil leaves, packed
1 teaspoon green peppercorns, crushed
1/2 cup light cream, heated
salt and pepper to taste
1 pound linguine

Cook the pasta in a large pot of boiling, salted water until *al dente*. Drain and serve with the following sauce.

In a skillet, melt the butter. Sauté garlic until lightly browned. Add the shrimp and scallops and cook over medium heat 5 minutes, until shrimp are pink and scallops opaque white. Add the basil, green peppercorns, hot cream and let simmer 5 minutes. Pour over pasta and serve immediately. Serves 4.

Twists with Chicken & Red Peppers

2 tablespoons olive oil
1 small onion, finely chopped
2 cloves garlic, peeled and chopped
1 whole chicken breast, skinned and
    cut into julienne strips
2 sweet red peppers, seeded, skinned and finely chopped
1/2 cup light cream
1/2 teaspoon Tabasco sauce
1 pound twists or any other short pasta

In a large skillet, sauté the onion and garlic in the olive oil. Add the chicken and cook over medium heat, stirring often, for 5 minutes until the chicken is lightly browned.

Add the red peppers and cook for another 5 minutes until soft and blended. Add the cream and Tabasco and simmer for 5 minutes more.

In the meantime, cook the pasta in boiling, salted water. Drain. Pour over the sauce, toss well and serve. Grated Romano cheese is a good addition. Serves 4.

Stuffed Cannelloni

Cannelloni can be made from either of two types of pasta: dried, cooked, split and stuffed or with fresh pasta dough cut into rounds or squares, lightly cooked and then rolled-up like crêpes or pancakes. Either works well for this recipe.

1 onion, chopped
1 clove garlic, peeled and chopped
1/2 pound ground veal
2 anchovy filets, chopped
1 teaspoon capers, chopped
6 oil-cured black olives, pitted and chopped
1 tablespoon chopped fresh basil
1 tablespoon extra virgin olive oil
1 egg
8 cannelloni
2 cups light tomato sauce
1/2 cup Parmesan cheese, grated

In a large mixing bowl combine the onion, garlic, veal, anchovy, capers, olives, basil, olive oil and egg. Mix lightly yet thoroughly. Use this mixture to stuff the cannelloni.

Place the pasta tubes in a greased baking dish, cover with the tomato sauce and dust heavily with grated Parmesan cheese. Bake in a 400 degree F. oven for 20-25 minutes until the pasta is piping hot and the cheese is lightly browned. Serves 4.

Shells with Vodka Cream

1 pound pasta shells, large or small
1 tablespoon butter
1 clove garlic, peeled and chopped
1 tomato, peeled, seeded and chopped
1/4 pound shrimp, crushed into a paste
1/4 cup vodka
1/2 cup light cream
salt and pepper to taste

Cook the pasta shells in boiling, salted water until done. Drain.

Meanwhile, sauté the garlic in the butter in a skillet. Add the tomato and shrimp paste and cook for five minutes over medium heat, stirring constantly. Add the vodka and let cook for 2 minutes to evaporate the alcohol and blend the tastes. Finally, add the cream and simmer for 5 minutes. Pour over the pasta and serve. Serves 4.

Pasta Primavera

There are a thousand-and-one recipes for pasta primavera (springtime pasta). The variety of vegetables depends entirely on what's available, but all should be young and in prime condition.

2 tablespoons butter or olive oil
2 cloves garlic, peeled and chopped
1 small onion, thinly sliced
1 cup mushrooms, thinly sliced
1 small zucchini, in julienne
1 small carrot, in julienne
1 cup broccoli flowerets
2 tomatoes, peeled, seeded and chopped
1 cup string beans, sliced lengthwise
1 cup asparagus tips
salt and pepper to taste
1 1/2 pounds linguini or other pasta

In a very large skillet or wok, heat the butter or olive oil (butter if to be eaten hot, olive oil to make into a salad).

Sauté the garlic, onions and mushrooms until soft and golden. Add all the other vegetables and toss over high heat until just crisp and hot. Pour over the cooked pasta and season with salt and pepper. Serve immediately.

If you wish to make a salad to be served at room temperature, toss penne with vegetables, add another 1/2 cup of olive oil and vinegar to taste and let marinate for an hour before serving. Serves 6.

Tortellini with Ham & Peas

Excellent tortellini, filled with either meat or cheese, can be bought in most supermarkets and specialty food stores. This makes a very rich dish, perhaps best served as an appetizer before grilled fish or meat.

1 pound tortellini
1 tablespoon butter
1 cup fresh shelled peas
1/4 pound prosciutto or good baked ham, in julienne
2 tablespoons olive oil
1 teaspoon freshly ground black pepper

Cook the tortellini in gently boiling, salted water as per directions on the package.

Meanwhile, melt the butter in a small saucepan, add the peas, cover and cook over low heat for 10 minutes.

Uncover, add the ham and heat through, about 5 minutes. Finally, add the olive oil and heat to just the boiling point.

Pour over the hot tortellini, sprinkle with pepper and serve at once. Serves 4-6 as an appetizer.

Pasta & Bean Soup

1 onion, finely chopped
1/4 pound bacon, diced
2 tablespoons olive oil
2 cloves garlic, chopped
4 cups chicken stock or canned broth
1 28-ounce can small cannellini beans
1 teaspoon hot pepper flakes
1/4 pound short pasta tubes or spirals

Sauté the onion and bacon in the olive oil, in a large
saucepan adding the garlic after 3 minutes. Add the
beans and pepper flakes and cook over low heat for
5 minutes stirring carefully (so as not to break the beans).
Add the stock and simmer covered for 15 minutes.
Finally, add the pasta and cook, uncovered until *al dente*,
about 15 minutes more. Serves 4-6.

Spinach Pasta with Shrimp & Mushrooms

1/4 cup olive oil
3 cloves garlic, chopped
1/2 pound mushrooms, thinly sliced
1/2 pound shrimp, peeled, deveined and cut into quarters
1/4 cup dry white wine
1 tablespoon fresh basil, chopped
1 pound spinach pasta (linguine is ideal)

Sauté the garlic in the olive oil in a skillet until lightly browned. Add the mushrooms and cook over high heat just until the juices begin to emerge. Add the shrimp and cook for 5 minutes. Now add the white wine and basil and cook for 2 minutes more.

Meanwhile, cook the pasta until *al dente* and drain.

Pour the sauce over and serve immediately. Serves 4.

Rigatoni Siciliana

1/4 cup olive oil
2 cloves garlic, peeled and chopped
1 medium eggplant, peeled and cut into 1/2 inch cubes
1 28-ounce can plum tomatoes, drained and
   coarsely chopped
1/2 cup seedless white raisins
1/2 teaspoon red pepper flakes
1 pound rigatoni

In a large skillet, sauté the garlic in the olive oil over
medium heat. Add the eggplant and continue cooking,
stirring constantly, for 5 minutes until the eggplant is
softened. Add the tomatoes and cook for 15 minutes.

Meanwhile, soak the raisins in hot water for 10
minutes. Drain.

Add the raisins and the red pepper flakes to the sauce
and cook for five minutes more.

Cook the rigatoni in boiling, salted water until *al
dente*. Drain. Pour the sauce over and serve. Serves 4.

Spinach Fettucine with Mussels

4 pounds mussels, scrubbed and debearded
1 cup dry white wine
2 tablespoons olive oil
1 clove garlic, peeled and chopped
2 onions, peeled and sliced thinly
2 carrots, peeled and julienned
salt and pepper to taste
1 pound spinach fettucine

In a large pot, place the mussels and white wine. Steam in a covered pot, stirring occasionally, until the shells open. When cool enough to handle, shell the mussels, reserving a dozen in their shells for garnishing. Strain the liquid from the mussels through cheesecloth and reserve.

In a large saucepan, sauté the garlic and onion in the olive oil until soft and golden. Add the carrot and cook gently, until soft. Season with salt and pepper. Add the shelled mussels and just enough of the reserved liquid to moisten everything to a depth of about 1 inch. Heat through, but do not let boil or the mussels will toughen.

Meanwhile, cook the fettucine in boiling, salted water until done. Drain.

Pour the sauce over the pasta and toss well. Garnish with the reserved mussels in their shells. Serves 4.

Ravioli Siciliana

This rather bizarre-sounding dish is actually quite good and mingles the flavors of Italy with the Arab-influenced cuisine of Sicily.

2 tablespoons pine nuts
2 tablespoons olive oil
1 large onion, peeled and chopped
2 cloves garlic peeled and chopped
1 28-ounce can plum tomatoes, drained and chopped
1 large can skinless, boneless sardines, preferably in
    olive oil, drained and coarsely chopped
1/2 cup seedless white raisins, soaked for 10 minutes in
hot water and drained
1 teaspoon hot red pepper flakes
1 pound small cheese-stuffed ravioli (available fresh
    at many markets and specialty stores)

Place the pine nuts on a baking sheet and toast for 10 minutes in a medium oven. Remove, cool and set aside.

In a large skillet, sauté the onion and garlic in the olive oil over medium heat, until soft and golden. Add the tomatoes and simmer, stirring occasionally, for 10 minutes. Add the sardines, raisins and red pepper flakes and simmer for 10 minutes more.

Meanwhile cook the ravioli as per the instructions on the package. Drain. Top with the sauce and serve immediately. Serves 4.

Pasta with Spinach & Sausages

1 tablespoon butter
1 clove garlic, peeled and chopped
1/2 pound sweet or hot low-fat Italian sausage,
    removed from the casings
1 10-ounce package frozen chopped spinach, defrosted
1/2 cup light cream
1 pound bucatini or penne

Sauté the garlic in the butter in a large skillet. When lightly browned, add the sausage meat and cook over medium heat, breaking up the sausage with a fork until lightly browned and almost reduced to sausage crumbs.

Add the spinach and mix well. Add the cream and let heat through.

Meanwhile, cook the pasta in boiling, salted water. Drain.

Toss the pasta well with the sauce and serve at once. Serves 4.

Orzo with Nuts & Mushrooms

Orzo is the tiny, grain-shaped pasta. It cooks very quickly and is perfect as a side-dish, to accompany roast or grilled meats.

4 tablespoons butter
1 clove garlic, peeled and chopped
1/2 pound mushrooms, roughly chopped
2 tablespoons walnuts or pecans, coarsely chopped
pepper to taste
1 pound orzo

Melt the butter in a large skillet. Sauté the garlic and mushrooms until soft and lightly browned. Add the chopped nuts and heat through.

Meanwhile, cook the orzo in boiling, salted water. This should only take about 5 minutes. Drain.

Toss the orzo with the sauce. Serves 4.

Rigatoni with Ragout

This is a dish to make when you are cooking a stew or pot roast (especially if flavored with red wine and herbs).

3 cups gravy from stew or pot roast
1 pound rigatoni
1/2 cup grated Parmesan cheese

Place the gravy in a small saucepan and cook over low heat, uncovered, for at least 1 hour, until the gravy is reduced to half its original volume.

Meanwhile, cook the rigatoni in boiling, salted water. Drain.

Toss the pasta with the gravy and 1/2 cup of grated Parmesan cheese. Serve more cheese on the side.
Serves 4.

Pasta-Shrimp Salad

1 pound medium shrimp, peeled and deveined
1 cup fresh raw peas
1 tablespoon chopped pimentos
3/4 cup extra virgin olive oil
2 tablespoon wine vinegar
2 teaspoons Dijon mustard
salt and pepper to taste
1 pound penne or ziti, cooked and drained

Cook the shrimp in boiling, salted water for 3 minutes. Drain.

Toss the shrimp with the peas, pimentos, olive oil, vinegar mustard and salt and pepper to taste.

Add the pasta and toss well. Serve at room temperature. Serves 4-6.

Farfalle with Peas & Bacon

1/4 pound pancetta or lightly smoked bacon, diced
1 clove garlic, peeled and chopped
1 cup fresh peas, shelled
3/4 cup chicken broth
pepper to taste
1/2 cup grated Parmesan cheese
1 pound farfalle

In a skillet fry the pancetta or bacon until the fat runs.
Add the garlic, peas and chicken broth and cook over a
low heat for 15 minutes, until the peas are tender and the
broth has reduced.

In the meantime, cook the farfalle in boiling, salted
water until *al dente*. Drain.

Pour the sauce over the pasta, add pepper to taste
and Parmesan cheese. Toss well. Serves 4.

Penne with Pesto

Pesto is the wonderful, uncooked sauce of Genoa and the Ligurian coast. There are dozens of recipes; all I can say is this one is authentic and good.

1 large bunch fresh basil
2-3 cloves garlic, peeled
1/4 cup pine nuts
1/4 cup Parmesan cheese or
    Parmesan and Romano mixed
1/2 cup extra virgin olive oil
pepper to taste
1 pound penne
1/4 cup melted butter

Place the basil (leaves only), garlic, pine nuts and cheese in a food processor. Cover. Process, slowly adding the olive oil until a thick paste is achieved. Add pepper to taste.

    In the meantime, cook the penne in boiling, salted water until *al dente*. Drain and toss with the melted butter. Place a spoonful of the pesto on each portion and serve with more cheese and butter. Each person mixes his or her own at the table. Serves 4.